AF472289

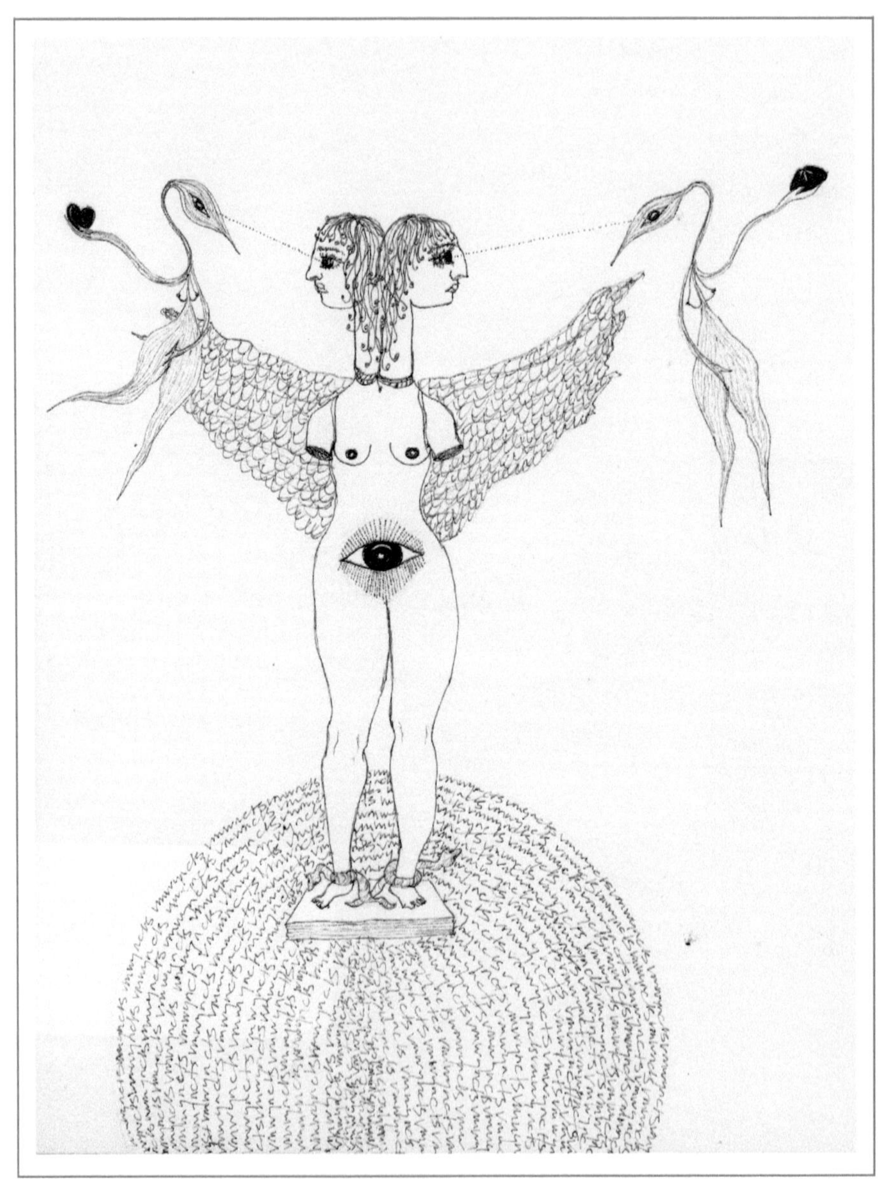

Untitled. Dolorosa. 2008.

A CURIOUS NIGHT FOR A DOUBLE ECLIPSE

PROSE POEMS

J. KARL BOGARTTE

La Belle Inutile Éditions

A CURIOUS NIGHT FOR A DOUBLE ECLIPSE
by J. Karl Bogartte

Frontispiece: Dolorosa

Published by Lulu.com

ISBN: 978-1-105-08313-6

La Belle Inutile Éditions

http://labelinutile.free.fr/index.html

A CURIOUS NIGHT FOR A DOUBLE ECLIPSE

“Waiting for centuries, a fabulous bird that comes into my desire, hatching a golden moment.” -Jacques Lacomblez

“I close my eyes, as active as a vampire, I open them within myself, as passive as a vampire, and between the blood that arrives, the blood that leaves, and the blood already inside me there occurs an exchange of images like an engagement of daggers. Now I could eat a piano, shoot a table, inhale a staircase.” -Ghérasim Luca

BOOK ONE

What is real, that does not pass through endless doors, in certain cities, at certain hours, continues for those who cannot help but follow even the most desperate solutions...

•

It was a night of beautiful effigies and transferences of raven-haired landscapes begging for your fingers, and everything around you was planting lucid dreams. The earth is humming... The capillaries of an inward planetary system are disrupting silence, changing course. All that remains bases its pleasure on the marvelous disarray of last minute decisions...

There is breeding in the immediate landscape, rich and elaborate notations that can only be deciphered by hand, by touch, or by mouth, pressed against the lips. A landscape for delirium. Radiant solutions for the beekeeper's seduction.

The meeting in the astronomy of arcane desperation. All the signs were rampant manifestations of a loving disposition to maintain the dimensions of passage and reconnaissance. The cinematic procession unfolding according to the vagaries of hallucination, and the world held tight to the forces of consciousness.

•

In the misery of short stories and cunning detours, where the grinding gears of pleasure interrupt the golden stones of night, the bridal chamber rebels against the salient features of a landscape nervously ticking and jealously blinking, and spinning like a top, and speaking in tongues to the phases of the moon.

There is no fable to the truth more telling than the one that is the imposition of the other, forming molten gestures, burning time; no truth of optics in the rain of ghostly arousal, nor in the sea reflection that suffers the hour of your braille and your double shadow, brightly seduced into sand and spaded through the whispering of unusual vowels. You die in yourself being born in the imagery of a flash flood, fingers forming the sun.

•

A bright and lingering pathology to the tales of fast moving windows caressed with your sex, and sidereal with only the lightness of images that lacerate the hordes sleepwalking through the shades that make you luminous in the richness of your gender, rich with uncut scenes moaning through unnerving libations and secret histories.

The eggs of consciousness are spinning for heat to announce the hunger of expressions. You feed on light. Tearing flesh for breath...

You are the she-enabled clavichord of feverish night-threes and evolving triangles, callous with each cognitive embrace that follows the jasmine-weaver's revenge.

•

Sunlight shares the blood that grooms you with smoke, following thoughtless shapes out of enchantment. Eye-soundings in the thought-black miasma of a swirling wake, the healing plasma that spreads your body over its absence. Strangers fine-tune their seeds and place them in small boxes made of moonlight. The marksman closes his eyes when the target stops to taste the wind...

•

She *among all of us, our twin* revolving like a sorceress of slowly spinning glass, through her identity of you along endless threads, and your acknowledgement of her (scaling towers), that turns each defining waterfall of light and shadow in the opposite direction, raising cane and masquerade, your brilliant means of escape... your owl's wing of desecration.

•

The perceptual conditions of her tree-minded flood, in the fullness of a cognitive ink spilled over everything at random, a stone's throw, brings her to mind as clear as a bell, a shameless razor fading into deep circles...

•

Light engages darkness and evolves, revolving. Clothing marks its territory with iridescent ashes. The apogee of a precise fall from a great height presupposes both the pain and the pleasure of a splendid disregard for acceptance. The minotaur's gown is hanging by a thread.

There is only an orphic solution to the meaning of one who feeds the other, ravishing the cinema of a lost stillness reclining in the naked clamor of thirst, forbidden the flower of release, the mint calyx submerged in the phantom of miraculous cures, from mouth to mouth, flowering in throats, in the glance that timeless tales tell of the scattering of the fabric, singing madly in a dream, and outside of it, in the forest, in the clock-tower of rain.

•

Now it is 3am, and it is always 3am when measurements are taken and placed in the empty living rooms where secret meanings are ebbing and flowing, evading the hair-threaders with their dangerous tongues...

•

That breath of darkness shaping and designing, it's shapes and designs casting a tincture on life that is the half of a broken key made of gold, on a back street in the imaginary center of Ecuador, where the old flute-maker discovers his astrological chart as a tree of thirst, in a forest of last regrets and migratory glances.

He, who leaves no trace of struggle or apprehension, imagines a formidable presence through himself without shadow, or doubt.

•

A phoenix-minded trauma, a cellular landscape of long-haired somatic dimensions spinning on the periphery of a trance, piloted by the fire of an entrance that dazzles the dark animal of a paramount tangent. She dies beneath the cloak of a loving fountain. You search her paws for clues, daring to leave the house only at dusk.

•

A night of glass-shaped bird memorials, with the witch growing more lucid with each kiss, each impossible arrival, never to be seen again except in darkness, when the tempting-machine begins to whir and spark with those obscene objects of desire flooding the empty rooms like salamanders and other grand gestures, other doorways.

Humor and cruelty conspire to overwhelm the hesitations of the flowering mink slowly ebbing into the curtain call of precocious masks and impossible solutions. Life has no answers, only marvelous distractions. Radiant equations.

•

Flying machines that bring the 12th Century back to its circles and distant relatives, perverse motors grinding up your shadow. *"Shh... If they hear us all is lost! If even a single movement breaks the spell, the Ibex of rapture will close the abyss. The thread of a miraculous dive will threaten the wishbone of her mouth in the fog of the speculator's kindling, and the wise men will die without ever knowing it..."*

Time is light spinning counterclockwise through your body. The checkmate is in the house of whispers and plundered for the pleasures of carbon and empathy coaxed into flesh, without slivers of memory setting blissfully in the east.

•

There was more to the language than a double eclipse. There were your hounds navigating the mirrors that preceded your attempts at casting doubt.

The game that is most intense when the apples come to glow, and the gifted hands of the translator fondle the abacus of distant fixations. A sudden dialectic mirrors the syrup of hallucination between the clothing of bereavement and the stairway that leads to the forest, and ultimately there is a devastating humor in the shadow when it ignites.

•

Earthly diversions and beautiful slashes that arrive before you, and live long after your departure, equals the light of constellations growing inwards: for the space of the language that forms your body, she is the mythology of your conjuring, the anti-culture of daring gestures and prolonged kisses, pulling milk-teeth out of mirrors inspired by the corset-menders and the silken armatures of Della Porta (the color of coral in a game of chance.)

•

The spirit of a forceful defiance, a dangerous rapture clinging to the parapets deer-laden with immaculate caressing sensations arriving fully formed, labyrinths of indecent exposures (Medea-roses) inciting curses and other idiosyncrasies, like sparkling lures or shining breastplates of adopted flight-patterns groomed as totems and delicious pets... Your mouth close to her ear, where the word *sinister* enters the mastery of jasmine and arson, like wind gathering the axial stones of consciousness into phantom arcades.

•

Often, there is the delicate cooing, the diabolical inclusions, the ravishing wishbones...

"Dearest Equinox, you must leave before the doors close in the children's eyes..." precise gesticulation to unsettle the savants in their hidden chambers.

The rare infernal flowers of locomotion, whispering amongst themselves...

A buzzing drama of dark machines and blonde pianos of a river that captures bells for pleasure and twitching, intimate with a street that follows the scent of your eyes. The magnolia of the wolf's eyes lit up like wounds seem like the grates of a sudden encounter, in the middle of the night, a flaunting image of pale mysteries torn into premeditated seductions.

"Equinox... out of the landscape, out of the forest, spin the fur into gold, into windows through stone, out of shadow spread your eyes into fleece... "

•

The anthropology of your body lives past the bronze age of those liquids that solarize the face of a woman, whose bell of slumbering shatters the city of elongated sorrows, and whose name in Galicia is venerated by scholars, and despised by children.

Her face follows rain and flood. Bones glittering for windows. Shadows cut into perfect squares.

Her name is always invisible, her gate covered with whispering, her fluids powering impossible getaways.

•

Soon the somnambulist mimes out in the garden will become statues when the sunlight arrives to breed and multiply, in the space of supreme values more dangerous than not, more fear-enlivened than merely shattering in the distance, between the edge of a knife still warm and the spilling of a disagreement in substance, the royal privileges of dissent among the seers assuming the stunning curve into hips of Spanish moss. A perverse inclination that breaks the circle of harmony and the vertebrae of mirrors, stalking perfection.

•

A dialogue knows only the limitations of desire and its children, and no rock formations are left to chance... although, chance was held in high esteem.

•

The bursting hive of perception releases the honey of a sudden revenge. An apocalypse of consciousness leaves you isolated and flawless. The ancient hamatsa of the heart strings together the confounding 0's and the enchanting 3's of those very first moments of the possibility of prevailing storms and enfilading fires in the antechamber of love's desperation.

To defile is the coming of wisdom. To sleep past the hour of paradise is a surprising molestation.

Life is another identity to the one you call your own, and the mystery of who desires its own form, follows the rush of nebulae...

•

The missing links ravishing the landscape, hesitant poses, reluctant portraits, the erotic gathering of phantoms that cast themselves skimming over the water, where you and your shadow mediate with death, shaking the clarities between the poles of unconscious desires, striking up the band, of thieves and precious stones, languorous nights collaborating with philosophers haunted by wolves in the foundry of priceless shoulder blades... Bone is like breath when it reflects the sun. It is like devotion, even when it slumbers and dreams of a desirable climax, a beautiful havoc no one can resist.

•

There is joy and longing in the skeletal remains of the astronomy that announces your passion, in quadrants, so completely out of step, so flint-like in those moments before waking, where you cannot even be seen...

"Eat me, my love, live on me with animal-thirst, in the charade of a diamond split open for perilous novelty. Lick my fleece and draw blood into enchanted circles... Suffer for me, my eager shadow, sip the nightshade of my buzzing and my antennae, and cling to my stake, glow for me in the shallows of all that resemble the artifacts of confusion and dismay... my love, enter me and become my hunger for you..."

•

Gold is time compressed into a diamond. Time is the process by which infinity lifts her dress just enough to unsilver the mirror that reflects your absence. Your breath is the completed triangle of a furious glance. Night trembles, because it knows you...

•

Desire and desperation unfold like roadblocks on a street of glaciers burning up the architecture of fear, where swans mimic giant prisms and autopsy implements fondling the brightest of your glimpses, with passion and concern, with empathy and idealization, a little violence and projection, a passing semblance of erotic devotion, and yes, filled with a certain grace, moments of acceptable doubt, an anguish that allows us to evolve... If we do not falter...

•

You are, in spite of yourself, a series of references, and ingenious designs, however brilliant and often too intricate for precise placement in the moment, and we become medial angles taunted by candles and poetic crimes in progress, crossbows of a lunar eclipse, and chaste fountains in the middle of the room with opened arms.

We follow you with intent to commit mayhem. We love you endlessly, your propellers tearing up the forest, and when your transparency astounds us, we love you even more.

A lunacy of longing dwells in us like words that have no meaning, but animal cries, torn linen, a loving defiance... There is hope for fire.

•

You surmount the "I" with numerous X's placed according to an identity stretched to the point of a feverish disinclination to return to the point of origin. You were never one to be trusted. Your notes were inspired, but fictitious. She was desired above all the others because of her mysterious refusals, her destinations.

In dark mountainous caves, life comes to meet you in moments of breathing gold through open doorways, consciousness inhaled.

Hunger was a pointing-stick implanting heat into eager statues, or dark-haired models who never spoke, harbingers of night passages found only in an exchange of nonsensical words between strangers, or shadows, merging.

•

The owl's mother was whipping up a mask for the aboriginal sleepwalker, the one who invented the seashore, where the water ends, where night is a magic potion, where water-wheels conduct the tides, becoming a moment of hesitation that colors every future gesture with the tenderness of claws. She had been gone for many years. Her shadow had turned into an umbrella. The rain would always come suddenly, and with her voice...

•

The agony of passion is the cat's-cradle of a dozen cities driven by desert winds at the speed of light, and she had left all that behind, for the harem-face and the enchantment of the species, the adorable poppies of language burning out her eyes... Only her perfume remains, the cold, hard diamonds of her scent. Her joy is ruthless.

"You will find devices of detection hidden among masons tools and bright hummingbirds, and your optical caresses light up like wet teeth..."

Clairvoyant cloth surrounds the bathing rituals for the witches, whose pauses are the wailings of sleep. They walk among us like spilled ink.

•

Celebration and seduction, a primal bottling of medusa-driven serums, where your reflection meets your shadow in a jealous quandary, and then reverses the direction of archetypal nods and pivoting stems and ocular roots in endless courtyards, beneath opulent gowns, across many languages, like flaws in the body of the universe firing up the antechamber of primitive delights...

The forest of uncertain devices comes to meet you halfway, offering caresses that destroy calendars and important dates, germinating only those poses that defy your own gravity. You might touch those who wander in close, in a spirit that lacerates the confusion of response, flooding empty rooms with precognition and long slender shadows bordering on irresistible lakes filled with final decisions and radical departures... but, as prey, beautiful and unerring... having seduced the predator with fresh indications of desire.

•

In your eagerness to kiss the statue of Isis-drawn seascapes trampled by radiant horses, the night bestows upon you the letters of love and conflagration, in one fell swoop, pulling up the sea and the hulking voudon-rose of gigantic leaps, spread out over a fictional terrain more real than your own. Your scent is a mirror that projects the opposite shore.

•

Your portrait is an unpretentious last minute glance that roams on its own through the city like an old belief system undergoing outrageous acts of metamorphosis and tender arcs giddy with auras.

Your reindeer cloak is sadistic with kisses, caged like precious unspoken hungers, dark murmurs glimmering in trees.

You drag the landscape along with your shadow, that raucous galaxy of unfinished evolution. Were you meant to be more than yourself, more than light, reflection?

•

You inspire sardonic and ambiguous aspirations. Your eyes spearheaded by kirlian steppingstones rising into vulnerable positions to oppose the uncertainty of intangible movements. Clues are always irresponsible, and without mercy.

The centrally positioned silence is preparing for rain, while the blood-flow of exhaustion urges the chandelier into a dance of dwarves and savage caresses giving off sparks and delicate farewells.

•

Exile is the diaspore of wondrous nights filled with radical conjunctions, glowing gestures: You slit the throat of a passing fancy that drops into a slumber and fades into the shaping of a horse-shoe under a loving hammer that betrays your presence.

•

There is a thrust of the cane, a twist of the hat, and the eyes reversed when the zookeeper's stroke of luck is a mad dash through the evening light, a fog of the dance in the shuffle of the cards, and an impossible stance, an engendering arc of pitch-black objectifies in the garden where the blindman's lantern hangs from its own light.

•

Sunlight is playing with it's captive fires, it's horrendous worlds distilled in orphaned shadows, and the phoenix is dreaming of your passage through a silvering language, in twos and threes, following fours and other unsuspecting numbers. Your enduring beauty is a reckless carcass more lolita-like in it's kindling than the dark of the moon, and littered with empathy.

There were secrets in the disparity of exemplary movement and those who swear by the pleasure of it. The rush of live wires igniting the memory of a present tense coming to light. Lunar branches...

Darkness nevertheless impersonates you, in reflection, between anxiety and unsettling susceptibility, and offers its breath, it's face, it's thirst, it's arousal... Invisible rivers, light years come to visit.

•

Her eyes are the scent of amethyst in the sudden recognition of a city on fire with the night. What she sees is the sound of that scent when the lights go out and darkness slips in close to lick her face. You spread her rapacious layers, severing the embrace of constellations from the horizon, and she opens her hive to harvest your desire for uncanny abundance.

•

The armatures of the marvelous, from which weapons are dispatched out of each well-placed act of transgression, are those indigenous totems of pyro-erotic playthings evoking stars that fill the rooms with whispering.

•

The genius that drives the objects of your affectations, seduces the simplicity of a reverse psychology, and compels the animals to explore the depths of your inquisition. The vanishing points bring a sense of living beyond your fingerprints and your outlines, your shadows (all of them) littered with wedding nights and possessive nights, nights of pollen and seeds dazzling with rare chemicals and gifts to undermine the flaws of possibility.

•

The word *arouse* deliberates in unseemly fashion, stalks the flight of stairs just ever so slightly above the phrase: *"There is nothing to question, only the light hovering in its cage"*, and life in the garden is rancid with constant trembling, a garden in a frenzy on the other side of the street, another world undreaming itself.

•

No one wanders the perimeters without slouching, or without lunar diversions tending to throw the scent like a voice across a lake, allowing for invisible passage. Rubbing females together produces a sound unlike any other, and always causes a sudden change of weather, like a hurried change of clothing, in the dark, in the middle of a recurring dream.

The shudder is a worthwhile key that never loses its balance, even in the most precarious locks, and still further, even while being watched by the most admired of Florentine craftsmen, you consider those prospects each night before fading, and consider yourself blessed, a dark horse.

•

Nights without equal, drooling light while the earth steadies itself, rising out of its depth to meet you; impossible nights, nights undone beneath the scalpel of empathy and antagonistic presence, making love to the gate of alternative endings. She watches you from leaf to leaf, in that light between shadows. Your signature is the suddenness of a swan.

Her sudden pose in the middle of a scene of rare exception, and without precedent, having disposed of the wealth of unforgiving ownership, assumes the rapture of a feeding frenzy. Reality is a doorway that mimics your reflection.

•

The peaceful co-existence of a shuddering pause and a profound mystery, fondling each other in a hazardous arcade, breathing sparks. The secret matter is gestating in the sadness of a girl, barely a grove of lilacs, almost, a pyramid.

•

Elegies are like antlers pushing through tender flesh, and the weight of your breath in the luster of an open window, pries apart the history of magic and science in the pain and pleasure of a moment outside of time. You have not consented to the limits of consciousness. You follow the river outside...

"Those fingers under my dress, those embers tearing out my flesh, that oracle of loving torments."

•

Only the rain understands the cooing of your eyes, and those miraculous glances that never end. A desperate act of defiance between two shadows.

Her eyelashes leading the way, the gyroscope of winds.

What strange words feverishly assault your presence in the swirling eddies of stone and touch, wind and exhaustion, the fire and the reflection, sea and conscious acts of purity, ash and senseless trembling, your violence in the rain calming the graceful ones buried in light.

•

In the coveted dimensions of love and madness the long-coated herons dive for the memory of those who disappear into lucid dreams.

•

There is a powerful thrashing of roots in the submissive nature of your scent disappearing behind you, storm centering in your awareness of being able to move outside of yourself, iron ore inciting the procession of primitive hallucination, sight mixed in sand, desperation of the moon under your skin, darkness bleeding stars and the blind woman grooming her serpents in the shame of candles, tears of charred wood, humor of glaciers and teeth, almost breaking, your movement through the air, in the pleasant derangement of an early afternoon.

•

All the masks have gathered together in the bed of sparks, long and slender quandaries, inseparable reindeer-orphans, raven-haired clairvoyants, circling overhead into the darkness of a violin-seeded field of wandering heretics...

"Your lips parted, the poisons flowering in the clarity of a poignant grappling, utterance acknowledged only by those who cease to hesitate..." and night is merely hovering above your tongue.

"When I offer those radiant demands, those flourishes, fireflies..." in those masks charmed by subterfuge and breathing separated only by desire, joined by distance and absence, arcane numbers, and swift retaliations. Your features defying gravity. Only phantoms bring rain.

The perverse pleasures of the captured bride dove-tailed in the mathematical equation of the city held up for example by the stars.

•

The earth is in the vessels divided by lunar riddles (the female wailing in the stables) and the destination of the King (the water of stars lapped by wolves) surrounded by the humming brides appearing and disappearing with the rapidity of ghosts...

Time ends in her bodice where mutations grow and flower, and the demands of each last breath tempts earthquakes into separating your shadow from your voice. The images you reflect, gradual points of entry, degrees of folly, ignited...

•

The apparition of forms is splicing the talons of longing into birthmarks, where the arrival of night-vision is arrayed in twos and threes: spindles in the servants quarters that orchestrate with all the joy of not one ounce of guilt, the silken train takes away the landscape and revives your presence in a form not unlike a gathering of unrelated reflections.

•

A doorway of visiting animals is your portrait for an architecture of blood, held together by vivid wind and stars, and the panting, shedding, multiplying, howling, making crystals of your exiled genealogy.

•

The Mares of Cappadocia are no less significant than the game of mirrors fending off the principles of cinematic projection. An attack of glow-worms. Your detachment ponders it's meaning, and reaches deep into dreamless beauty...

"It is believed that identity translates into a city of spell-shaped moments of precognition... the rest: a sorcery of reflections."

The forge delivers veils that stop at nothing. The movement of intense voyeurism outside of conscious hybrids equals the fondling of one by another who knows your weakness, for pleasure, for perfection, strikes your curves and ambiguities, and alters your landscape.

•

Your chemicals build passages in stone the color of a lake spelled: *obsessive*... and for that reason, you dive deeper than light and strike an arc for your illusion. You leave under peregrine pretenses, numerous personas, defending the passion between humor and desire.

Ravenous objects rebel and hunt for attractions.

•

From the moment of your waking, when the light comes silently to you with it's offerings, your perception translates into gears and armatures, mechanisms of birdlike fluidity, and all the secret matter of the mind's immersion in that one female shade that disappears through any door that assaults you... glowing, attracting, a ruthless lure. Even the movement of lead in its heaviness is a golden glow bordering on intimacy. A lyrical synesthesia.

The intense gaze is the zodiac of a blind wizard when he balances precariously between the mannequin and the candelabra, divining for desire.

•

Darkness burns mazes into the avenues where your solitude nests, unveiling the youthful siblings of uneasy inventions, seductive ciphers and vague spyglasses whispering endearing phrases... the cello attracts rival veils and slips of the tongue.

Lovers, merging in the fog of feral utopias, mumbling priceless words tearing membranes.

Darkness lowers itself through the heart-valve of vicious children, diamond-yielding sparks performing for the pieces of the puzzle that pose ever so delicately above the waking, and those who enter the wake.

The invention of night, the ageless question of impossible balance, the pilot's daughter eating crystals: To fill the world with light, the void with imaginary bodies glowing in the dark...

*

The ancient horned flower of your psyche attracts the devoted milking machines, the aboriginal veins of a fabric that propels your footsteps as determined as her threads slipping into light, vanishing in the blink of an eye.

•

The perfect alignment through the axis of it's twin, quartered and shelled in the gasping for breath and emerald, adored and pandered for pleasure and sight unseen, she licks herself in meadows of ermine and chimera, aching, angelica posing in the likeness of her bees sipping, through every sense of pulling ravens out of her body for kindling.

Dark gravitational assignations seduced into amulets the color of glass, evolving in sequential chiaroscuro, tempting blood where (in the Manor of Sighs) the barbarian sign-language seizes the images of your being in the rich, antiquarian lucidity of your extinction. Your face, or the features of night in the fever of graceful spirits that still come to drink the liquid of life out of your hands, the pendulum... An evening of theater runs ahead...

•

The weapon you most cherished was feminine. The wedge forced into the appearance of things was ambiguous with its dark insistence and wind-up astronomy, clicking and whirring about in circles and broken up by triangles into long, interminable caresses that went on forever, imitating a newly discovered galaxy quivering in the nearness of wolves.

Flight is only the body torn by light, and powered by obscene gestures. A choreography of wish fulfillment.

•

There is only the daughter of Icarus, without mirrors, the shadow of uncertainty that surrounds the ribcage of a philosophical paradox, only the stone of a primitive light, only the glance that hatches in the fire, the optical mainspring of a science that runs amok, only the ciphers leading the fossils of daybreak, and the glowing of those beings you feed each morning, the pools of blood dripping out of your dreams.

•

There is always the diamond-cutter's unremitting caress, always those great moths entering your eyes in a frenzy of unconditional attraction, clearing a space for the ermine of humor, and the misplaced objects of great value.

You have left the shape of your absence lingering in the wedding night still ravaging the city, still gesturing in the air, invisible ink making the anatomy visible.

•

Among the various diversions and unforeseen discoveries, when the shallow end of a gesture foreshadows a long and hazardous recovery, and sudden landings in desolate places, it is your eyes most of all that appear as an interlocking resolution, or the honor among thieves.

•

The rocks are dark with doorways in the landscape. Darkness is a knife sharpened in the purity of a loving proximity, to the otherness of pleasure, the childless candle, the animal stirring in sleep, the reflection poisoned by love.

You have left the shape of your absence lingering in the wedding night still ravaging the city, still gesturing in the air, invisible ink making the anatomy visible.

•

But, *"whose face is this? Whose eyes?"* The sinister grace of lucid numerals that pierce this façade of sleep. Whose shimmer dissolves the hesitation, the gold's apprentice, in what ape-veil comes the marvelous constellation? Your expression is that which collects the rain and dissects the struggle between the reflection and the shadow in a torrent of memoryless spaces, moaning of love.

Whose face, that doorway, a nest of spiders, a hemorrhage of stars...

•

She is licking blood off dusk, humming eyes through waves, a throat of glowing and wet ashes, that breath of timeless thirst, that abandon and delirium stirring up hiding places in lost glances... She was not to be trusted, but found in flagrante delicto in a conscious valley visible through her body, in the melted wax, inhaling life and light from a secret lake, exhaling the prisms in the animal's sight, the lunar visions from a deeper place.

•

She crawls with a most unusual grace, another presence in the room, always thirsty, always hungering. She follows the assassin, caresses his ancient totems. Her touch is a killing sense of direction, a magical captivity in time, in possession of every key. The veils of splendor torn by enchantment.

•

Lepidoptera and cinnabar for the walls and the lookout towers, the fool's hat and the passive flower for the models that beckon from the virgin's forest, the mummy's scarf for the summoner's apprentice sleeping with the owls, moving mountains, keying the locks, untelling the royal moves into occultation and river mining, pulling precious stones out of blindness. Consciousness is the little death of presence, tearing off the petals one by one for the structure of the wishing-bone that mimes the city, in the flood of memories not your own. *"I am, I am not, I am, I am not... Are we?"*

Love with knives under the loupe of recognition, the murmuring of auricles far from any street in any shadow or reflected in any mirror, far from the fluttering eyelids of tremendous contrivances.

"For love, little one, there are the statues of mirage, the fire-stalkers and their siblings, the forlorn ones, the forgetters, and the forgers, those noctambules wavering on the ladders of anguish in a moon calendar marked against defeat, and moving very fast..."

•

The radical purity of the interloper clothed in the spyglass of a lost continent, a sepia-toned quality of child-like weaponry poured in molten glass through a receding landscape. She is not available for consultation without the espionage of the morning dew, the bright poisons settling over the black shale beneath the female seduction of a brilliant whisper.

•

When the magician conjures the appearance of a mythical presence, which on the outside is the darkness of a fountain in the middle of the body, and on the inside, in another landscape, another language, the phantom object of a predator and a prey locked in a most unusual and splendid dance...

•

The autobiography of a charlatan, snake-charmer, hypnotist and object of pleasure who was lost in the undersea currents, leaving only a faint scent that can't be recognized, a collection of earthen jars without origin and numerous scribblings in a foreign tongue. Impeccable explosives, hurried kisses defeating the hour of sorrow: these were the definitive rumors, the beginnings of a captain's log. A sentiment of intrigue, a buried treasure... A sea of stars in a mountain matrix, hissing. Your suit of armor.

•

Each of your gestures is an echo, each one of your movements, titillating armatures of the imaginary collapsing the city into explosive cubes of what can be seen, when least expected, but desired above all else, a devastating urgency, thrashing imperatives threaded with ether and foam-riddled sphinx-agitated bodies: there is the humming system of circulation exceeding its masquerade, passing through the beguiling images of naked and empty stairways, to carry your blood from one aquifer to another. Flowering in the desert, with missing links, killed by beauty.

•

At risk, perhaps only your life, the mantis of eager principles and the poetics of an unforgivable misfire, the wires unhooked, shuttles advanced, totems caressed and released: at the most, a precise curve of the spine, when the solstice of a glance strikes the stone of craving images, breathing marrow and light into negative dimensions.

Your weapon of choice, the body of fire. Precious gems given free passage.

•

In the chamber of the bride, the King mates with the shadow of her reflection, and the creatures in the Game of Night are playing with their fears. There's nothing sacred about it. Just the animals playing, the fabric feeding a simple fire, teeth tearing flesh.

•

She knows the weight of her death, the color of it and the condescending poppies of her fields slashed by the lightning of consciousness, that breathing of other desires, the splashing eddies of crime-stone voyages, fur-shaped star-clusters acknowledging the name and identity of your bright and heraldic dance.

You have mingled with her for centuries through flawless histories, brought her back to life, twin of light in the abyss of the mirror. Fables running wild... The migration of arrowheads for the dew-sparks of agonizing words, spilled at random for phantom eyes.

•

In the evening cloth, precious as the bell-ringer casting an oval thought long since lost to ambiguous gestures, she is a hidden distillation, an endless flow of mint out of the forest. The spirits of the hour bring her shadows for fanciful assaults, and visions with bright names running ahead of each evasion, each gait and footstep she releases. The reindeer adore her, and the ravens whispering her reflection: *"keys to... keys to... the lake..."* and the antlers make her face, sorcery of the rain igniting flowers, breaking windows out of mystery, *"keys to..."* the act of changing course, against darkness, gambling for sudden targets, *"the lake..."*

•

Perception is a liquid extracted from approaching apparitions.

The bride ennobles the assassin, the wind defeats the sundial of sorrow.

Silence antagonizes the concept of arrival, pulling light out of the tiger's mouth.

•

The levels of consciousness passing through at unfamiliar angles, aroused by intuition and the enfolding future of wasps in a secretive handshake... The word for venom is always glowing in the dark.

The storm takes your shape, impregnates those clear-cut moments of primitive bliss and darkens them. Everything unknown comes from deceptive distances. Authenticity enlightens death.

The molecules coming together, for a few moments, timeless, pure attraction without rhyme or reason, images without names...

•

Setting up a precarious relay of lunacy and perfectly chiseled spring-times, the mimosa in a rampage, veiled antagonism of the water-gathering archway, your slipping naked and unafraid through the ancillary fleshing of mirrored substances, in the vice of bathing, and the watchman's sister branded with stained glass and absolute weightlessness... a psychological flaw that follows a change of attack, a means of rejuvenation.

Her eyes keyed into your weakness, laying the flint of distraught curtains raging war against the obvious, pulling broken geodes out of heavy breathing.

•

The sound of blood opening windows, distracting a melancholy plumb-line that swings from one moment to the next, in the tincture of centuries, a perfect groping sensation of invisible numbers.

Your philosophy fills a gypsy shawl with the labyrinth of pleasure, a burning building guided by other realities towards another meaningless doorway... The shadow of consciousness touches you... There is only the urge to lucidity without numbers...

•

In the gown of intricate tripods, the motives unleash their cities, stone-lighted thirst rapidly advancing, the dog-faced enchantress of night-blooming solar flares, of a sliding scale propped up against the harp strangled by a parachute.

The sense of multiplication, flesh that glows out of the eggs that circle the dark alleys of a psyche that knows only the desire of its twin, the oval mirror that repeats its garden in the exhaustion of moon after moon, within moon, pouring...

•

Amazed, there are she-creatures darting through imperfect doorways. Cambrian tremors paused in your flesh tones and just below your eyes, where she leans in before passing through artifice, a night of raptors and the whispering of interpreters, the siren of melted candle wax trowels that gamboling dive through empty streets, with the interlopers of fugitive beauty and perfected gestures of sinister grace, your waking state, your identity... traces of your illusion scattered to the four winds...

Angular and moth-like, endearing scalpels creating music for empty clothing.

•

The delicious cocoon flowers through the telescope of distinct conversations, severing its glow from the clock's pendulum during an evening stroll, on the verge of becoming hermetic and surrounded by blind men with their second sighted companions, those sudden keys of revelation and the nursing herons, those eyes surrendering to the slaughter of the aurora in her long, tedious coat... her stockings shedding light at the entrance, filling up with sap as amorous as senseless dialogues in darkness... bathing the silence of a dream.

•

"In a moon calendar marked against defeat, and moving very fast..." She is severed from her body (the horns of a dilemma...) rich in the dancer's receptacle of chartreuse and the possibility of statues. Flattering the depths into which one branches out, at once immaculate and disheveled, a thread of utmost possibilities pulled taut between two warring tribes... a pool of equal division. There must first be the life within lived by others, and loved by fire, over-reaching to be seen, in the mystery of similarities... then life unknown, followed by desire.

The hours burning up in the forest, hypnotized by humming, scattered by light. Life without words, or ashes on water?

BOOK TWO

Desire is the glow of apes, the furnace of a child and the eyes spinning in reverse.

•

Invisible gestures. Leaning in closer than anticipated, for a spell of pleasure, a female key in the embedded folds of anticipation, a surprise ending. In clairvoyant fields she is overseer of the kingdom of veils, but only, if and when, you decipher to intrude and deny yourself the freedom of thoughtlessness. The sound that ambiguity makes when it settles into the fog, slender-bodied, long-haired and filled with windows... Love threatens the unnatural peace of claws toying with eyes.

•

The planetarium of dusk, a ghostly ship of unknown origins, interpreting the hair of certain women; the dust accumulating in the blouse of restlessness, where your objects remain suspect and immoral, (blowing glass...) in a much disputed grand fashion, each venture into portraiture yielding the appearance of yourself, neither here nor in passing, yet endlessly appearing... to appear beside yourself, le prisme de l'être, the three-headed King, to disappear.

The doorway of mortality is the mask of feverish philosophers.

•

Eureka is night stalking, she aches for its blood, the passive streams, threading arteries through the needles of deaf-mute determination and tormented youth. The voyeurism of deception with a touch of painful tenderness, the tongue of a violin that embodies a curse. She is groomed because of her stature that influences the rotation of distant planets. Beneath your lids of twilight are placed the puncture wounds of unanswerable thirst. Prowling...

•

The assaults... To exceed where nonsense favors sudden fires. The shadowing of your psychology in the phosphorous that beguiles where language comes to entangle and breed, breath out of words that precede your arrivals filled with time. In this strolling of encounters turning antlers in the direction of a woman sipping life out of circular shadows, there is only the astronomer, in pieces, moments of gazing and wrenching death out of inwardness, a handful of wandering sparks.

Perception arcs between bones. A bright body between wolves.

•

Silence is amorous between words, between worlds, desire with its sparks and fabric that weaves around a desperate attempt at purity's dark, confusing ebullience. The hibiscus of phantoms, in the tunnels of El Morro, keys are hanging from her lips, in the convexing mirror of the lighthouse bride.

•

A revolution of women follows the night and the eves of harrow, and nothing returns from the rain. The thrones are reversed. Facial expressions changing spaces, reversing places with the rising sea. The chappell of ladders fuels the breath-earths in their clamoring, their knife-colored eyes and lips, those experimental armories, in which no light fears its heart-breaking twins.

Each image aroused is a monumental procession. A splicing of worlds too unknown to be known, at a depth barely pierced, a perverse navigation aroused into childlike abandon, as memory becomes insignificant. *The gnashing of nebulous tattoos...*

•

Armatures of light and water conspire for the warring tales, a bright spirit made of wolves, a throat in the fountain of analogies.

•

In the hourglass of ravishing and salvaging the very distinctions that delight between the window and mirror, between the battlefield and the exquisitely formed les petites morts with their wind-blown shutters and violet nights, when the worker-bees plunder the half-sleep tales of the heroic suit of armor plunging deep into the miasma of an imaginary conflict. The dance itself is filled with eggs when the moon brushes out the languishing of inspired games, each egg placed according to the vagaries of pain and pleasure, attractive disasters, whims, brilliant exposés. A disheveled incantation...

•

The horned gown of the mythographer mates the Queen of squalor in the nest of her pathological emeralds, baffling mirrored images, setting the depth-charges of lakes in motion, where grappling with everything invented reverses its course, where glass comes to meet you from vaguely remembered dreams, where evenings in Genoa conspire with poetic demands, and the unapproachable attractions giving off the scent of jasmine and pine and veiled oranges dripping endorphins and ripening equators assembled in abandoned warehouses, for your delight, alone, unmeasured, unrestrained...

•

Devious motors whipping space into entrances... In your illusion only reality pilfers those unmerciful curves and angles, passing through while capturing the flow of molecules, offering that single, obligatory rose, that comical tilt of the head, the flippant delay (while the earth spins wildly beyond control...) and the possibility of moving in closer than even breath allows, exchanging blood, identities, visibilities.

•

"If I touch what arouses you, will I conceal all that reveals your absence, and if I deny you your illusion, will you crave my departure and the wilderness that replaces it? Will that pleasure be enough to sustain your equilibrium, enough to keep you alive? Will words without meanings ever define for you the stillness of my desire... enough to dismantle your desire for me? Can you live within me, outside of yourself?"

•

Aberration of veils expelled. The antlers of your chest, expanding compass. Bones of lightning balanced with speech. Bride-powder scattered in wind. Coarse abundance... Witches stirred up with starlight and despicable auguring, as lovely as dripping candle-wax on delicate spirits drawn by intuition to the brightness of your hunger.

The stuttering of immense moths driven by adoration and eagerness, releases the psychological pomp of boar-fluted throwing-knives that linger above your sleep, designing magnetism for astounding images. The sleeping otherness, the sleep-enthralled other ones collared to the woof and warp of somatic messages written in darkness.

An ordinary evening, so it seems, settles in the mountains where ghost-writers come to shape the dead, merely languishing...

•

The ultraviolet of precious alloys (disfigured tigers, a blindman dreaming, ashes), reverberate like precious eyelids swooping down over naked acts of stolen kisses that mask the season of reflections. Purity reigns like a sudden storm.

•

The means of perception, like eager widows, prefigure the archrivals of illusion, and settle the score with enraptured appetites and barely visible sparks, enough to turn the tables into elaborate schemes worth a fortune in hallucination.

Perception reclines and unravels itself, drawn by echoes and esoteric principles resembling bell-towers seen from ravens and other time-caressing sibyls that pursue you and attract feverish identities.

Vampires like dolls clutching children with skin of porcelain lamps. Your noble presence was profound, and she, the long moving cloak of dawn, offered you sight-unseen, the wishing bone of a long-haired decision, a lit fuse of unthinkable streams, an ancient light.

In the woods where the roulette wheel unleashes its sovereign costumes...

•

Rattling horns, a soluble movement. The anesthetic of a rendezvous based on the liquid aspects and membranes of perception, gathered among orphans and various personae as heavy and beautiful as the manacles of a lesser power (a tiny but splendid conjuration) that none-the-less flowers in the déjà vu of multiple random games. Sudden particles sharing the sense of vast expanses meeting in the blink of an eye... and eyes closed in the exactitude of discovery. Intimate gestures of fire, ravaging the stone of discontent. Memory is the veil of time.

•

It is in the curve of her gathering, where the playthings of enchantment pull the strings of her seductive merging solution, that unfathomable abacus of germination. You lick her milk from the mouth of desire, an early morning ritual, a moment when here and future congeal, between now and then, solarized among the objects of power.

That guise of emerald from which a pure breath emerges, beneath the words *"I ache for the dive that prevails among the feverish games, those mercurial blue glances, the wailing keels, and that splendid archway sunk like exquisite corpses shimmering among the pines... sunlit pharmaceuticals, spoon-fed acrobatics... I know intimately the shadows that suffer for your pleasure."*

Primal light of streams, light-hunt and gathering. The sleepwalkers long swaying coats following the pathology of owls, striking the flint of the moment of your birth that has always defied the dark, arduous passages, held up to the light in the most sadistic way. The most desirable attractions held prisoner in the most encouraging word: soluble... governed by silence and desperation, the landscape bright with spirits that know your curious shape, and the silhouette that precedes it.

Spires, the color of breath. Her presence, the invisibility of wind.

•

The haunting of language, on a balcony, at the edge of consciousness where statues breed with unsettling cleverness, singing softly to themselves.

The blood on her lips is the flower between yes and no, the sudden spark in the courtyard, the impulse to move the center of gravity outside the body, beyond the central means of escape – the mind as hard as stone, through which can be seen the windows of time, the endless colonnades of a disfigured embrace, a word to the wise, a confluence of rivers to confound the means of perception. She drinks the fever of life. Her thirst is as pure as the infinite gaze of a voyeur. Her gaze from the mirror... in your eyes, the horizon.

•

In the lapidary stillness of anything that resembles desire, surefooted glances burning up the fullest measure of nighttime's most fearful undoing, lethal endgames...

•

In the kiln of quizzical utterances, the Antelope King is dissolved in the words of love, in sinister and in blindness, in disarray and quicksilver, in death and in crystal, in despair and murmur and in blackness, in solstice, and loon, the nightly bloom of the evening girl's endlessly multiplying flower, a conflict of angelic theories, in the coven, a telepathic reversal of mythical proportions, the *"eager widows"* of unreason, the ferocious irony of that one moment of an eternal presence in the process of dissolving, the hour released in the hand of dust, the kiss of the phoenix...

•

Draped in the exile of a fountain, the aggressive pendulum of X against X in the hive of emerging portraiture, the central nervous system of constellations for an essential foreground of irresistible elements, and a backdrop of nomadic departures, her skull is glowing through her skin. Against that unknown quality your appearance is a reckless clamoring that raises the question of a silvering of sudden languages torn out by their roots.

The recurring image throws a curve. A double eclipse burning with tulips that dislodge the aurora from the eyelids of absurd conjectures. You are suspended in the evening wax...

•

The life of a savage caught up in penetrating the reflection in the mirror, of that life, and those lives that radiate in unfinished plundering in that immense purity and nakedness, of reflected surfaces following the ashes of a bridge, where those figures loom dripping down over the edge (over that one river in which you were born), and the ribcage of turbulent galaxies liberated by the number of days in each month dedicated to the hummingbirds of intuition... and amulets gathering words into weapons.

•

The fear of misalignment leads to an Ojibwa of swiftly arriving objects, devoted to antediluvian hieroglyphics and uncertain sexual ecstasies that rival the measurement of time. Reality begins to grow the elements of your desire.

"Ojibwa, separated by impossible mornings, in the forests of love and solitude, refining gold..."

•

Marvelous vestiges, apothecaries of anything that resembles desire. Assyrian names written on whispering paper, the body is light swimming through words... and in the courtyard where snakes playing fiddles for the statues from another era, having only just arrived, form the landscape of a lassitude more personal than childhood discoveries that enter the costumes of foreshadow and depth of field, in the central brightness of a lit fuse. The disquieting block and tackle of the warrior's perilous flight.

•

A raging silence condescends to pass between *each other's* lips, charred words, miracles of light scaled by epochs of mystery, blood, spilled, swallowed, the scent of spirits colliding in invisible doorways, wind, rousing a tumult of crystals rearranging the mesa, the living plaza, reenergized by dizzying periods of night and day, in the folds, inclusions (formless objects) of vitreous fluids, habitually magnetized, chlorophyll and rain, of silk and needles' eyes, together, mixed with the confrontation of wolf and woman, in the calculated risk of strangers, mostly blood and spirit, mostly bright poisons, measured immeasurability, seeds (cut by knives dipped in dream) bathing in fire. You claw triangles in the air, blind-folded.

•

The rose is ruined upon the table of her knees, that milky substance of the spider's bite... where the surface of devoted water invites the phantom indices to equestrian disorder.

•

"I would not die for your dismemberment, for you, but kill for your steadfast gaze, that illusive barge swinging among others of otherness too prolonged by ether to deny their attractions... My thrones are empty for your deceptions. My weapons incur the voodoo dolls of a fawn-covered mirror..."

A tincture among spells, reality breaks with its opposite.

"I am not, whole, once again, but the salamander's path."

•

It is not the cocoon, nor the pollen that dazzles the mind, gathering handfuls of precious stones filled with the sparks of sleep and embezzlement, but the ascendant flood, the helicoptering of a great allusion to a paradise that showers you with the abyss, your breath fluted by consciousness through the mouth-mask of sentient encounters. Illustrious gears of howling, murmuring, bodily tremors signifying the defense of metamorphosis, no matter the cost.

The friction of accident between the hero and the heroine, and the watchman's absurd passion for the great pyramids in the shawls of young women. The objects of your fixation are swimming, devoured by manticore myth, the old woman turning the lathe...

•

She is visited by light, and chambered by perceptive doors, and she spirits the breath that foreshadows entrance into earth backwards. She enters the visibility of a luscious discontent of frenzied rubbing and water arched in its own system of spells cast in the windup universe of an outrageous dance.

•

You lower yourself to lick the stem of her transference, inhabited by presentiments of touch and idiotic proportion. A door-like paradox of double-time, a dazzling amalgam in navigational speech, tied with preemptive strikes to the horizon... She, the other one, generates telltale embers beneath the mouth of adamantine and cinnabar. The elder pose is a dark gown of perfect likeness. Sun fades to river, imitates anthracite.

•

There is, in the nacreous petals of your aspirations, a nomadic and very black alchemy that increases the enchantment of a loss of memory. Direction fluctuates, but it was never into the center that the wind carries its bright self-propagating hermetics, but out of the center into all directions, the plenary form in the solar bride, polar incest of shimmering intelligences rising out the earth's peripheral cabinetry, pandering-machines of loving madness...

In the still crawling of widowing balance, night-dust is spiraling the moment you realize your presence is not singular.

•

Noontime is the arrival of diverse mechanisms that set the muttering-machine into the motion of a starry morning's flood of illicit moorings, hobbling gratefully in a purity enforced by ancient weaponry, a lavish system of exceeding reach, grasped one through the other, from each other, where blood is transparent, and the quiet exaltations of aleatory conquest implant mutations into each word spoken alive, each word swallowed.

•

The tongue penetrates, hunger devours the essence, and the candle of a sinister fabric plunges your face into a plaza of bones made of dawn. The velocity of playful motors reminiscent of reclining plumage...

Love between phantoms... the elder humming that tilts every visible field into countless misconceptions, breathing shadows...

•

Pleasure is the arc of the prey, the intuitive gravity of unsettling chimerical jolts and fondling, the horns growing inward across a central field of delirious wonder.

•

There is nothing evident, or filled with milk where everything seems to be invented, or riddled with envious gestures that dislodge the cruelty of innocence to be reflected backwards in time, for only a twinkling, passing through permutations of possible scenarios, changing the notice of a moment. A mad dash into mirage, the castle dismantles the lucid perversions of its leading lady into the keyholes of dawn.

•

Darkness is an ovulating gesture; light is somnambulance in fierce tandem with identity.

•

The biology of your body is a starry arcade on an empty street somewhere in another place, resolving a mysterious woman who resembles a jeweler's sleepless night, a chemin green with rivers held up by serpents and desperate measures...

You see her in the double consciousness of a two-way mirror, spinning the silk of a dream that holds the city intact, a city of sleep and warm solutions to the ever-present intrigues of the bearded lamp hallucinating it's own means of travel.

The northern atmosphere devised a web of amorous dimensions. She withdraws the moon from your attractions and plays with them: *"I love you like a soundless bell ringing..."*

•

Purity very seldom casts suspicion. The structure is an eager fire, a furious and insatiable one. Always, at the correct moment, your posture reflects unnatural configurations of restlessness, a snipers' invisibility, a childhood game.

There is the perfidious clamoring of doll parts and expensive time-pieces rearranged according to the velocity of poisoned darts, the whispered and shuddering distractions of appearances and cruel adaptations... In this, the sadness of a swan in the center of a crime, the fingerprints of a possible seduction.

•

"I cannot be seen during moments of conflagration, but a consultation is always a threat, a developing condition preceding an act of passion and surrender, a savage caress..."

The psychology of objects becomes an understanding of unconditional desire. Your slumber is a desperate ruby caught up in the solicitations of an evening without forcible entry, offering only the chance to succumb to the idolatry of an exquisitely unfinished kiss like a phantom limb. She speaks only with her tongue slipping between obsidian and penumbra. Hers is the gothic tree laying its eggs in the psyche of a lost passageway, where shadows are swimming with pleasure; your breath flows through her leaves.

•

The mask of an animal nature pierces you with its tuning-fork, releasing the perfumes of a dangerously alert and fashionable sorcery, the nuptials of an enfilading net, sojourning... You search for her presence among the rocks, the black solar triangles of volcanic liberties taken, and predict a lyrical succubus gleaning the fire hibernating in the water, foraging for a flint as feminine as a feast, scaling the cabal of captivity and aroused anguish fumbling in the dark, shimmering in Jivaro symmetries, enough to make you tremble, to make you glow, enough to double the significance (with regard to time) of your own clairvoyant proportions.

•

With an acute gesture of friction and an almost painful sense of tenderness, the milky way cuts with a knife freed of inhibitions... and you cannot fail to question the critical aspects of a catastrophic blue, to announce an amazing descent into the dreams of others, so unlike your own, yet so similar in tone, with your rocking-horse, your dreaming threads, and the silent resuscitation of your shadow, caressed by secretive and long drawn-out reflections. Your name minus the sound that it makes when it hunts, claws extended...

She seems like you, that complex shadow, in significant alignment with the heart of murmuring in the forest, under streams that coalesce in the eyes... and yet, she is the dust of your ancient glimmering, the rapid eye movements of a cherished voyage that is abandoned for a game that wins and explodes, that spreads out into numerous vanishing points.

She is the hybrid of color and scent welding the air of tungsten and instinct to the hovering brood of a landscape that fleshes out your autobiography, one caress after another, one single ripple followed by others, water into water, separated into a prism of hard brilliant light,

•

Conduits and constellations, the barbarism of your voice. Capillaries and tributaries, sliding into prominence, fluxing and fusing. The shoals of both visible light and dark siren unmask in the masquerading of conscious thought, the inclusions of extra-sensory recognition. Into those rebellious waters diving comes to meet you.

•

The moth-making stone of uncanny cultivation, your seeing-eye candle. *"To the spirits of night, a girl again among fireflies..."*

•

Night is a bride stripped of her crystal, a facetted marsupial of desperate measures.

•

To ovulate in Latin, you must first place the object against it's opposite, setting fire to its task: an erotic liberation of objection. A crucial balancing act between distinctions, where the animal and the spectre resolve their intangible bodies, to engage their threads of reciprocating uneasiness.

A pathology of distant splendor, an evolving visage of desirable manifestations, the body as honey, the hive as presence and absence in sustained union, the bees of light circling...

•

The medicinal routes, the mummified streetlights, an agonizing farewell that braces for a medieval plague, the prose of a spell, blind reconnaissance...

Without question, it is a poetic spirit that works the weapon, that crafts and binds the forest of appearances, and the oneiric language of waking up unknown and beside yourself.

Hidden in the minor arcana of a troubled sentence, a whispered entreaty, a careless spell... a groomed horse beneath the bride.

•

In the mirror of your interior body, where random sexual ecstasies are crushed like peaches and spread out over the ramparts of an unfounded city, a window is planted, carbon smashed, leaking alchemical transgressions. The knowledge of amethyst darkens her lips... The need to speak has vanished.

•

A double shadow of lost tribes painted with tribal inklings that border the anterior of an always unfinished axis, that brings a sense of living into the walls littered with the heaviness of that infernal swaying, that ricochet of *yes* and *no* into *other* and *then* that lands in a field of transparent welders, scarring the lapis of a flaw in the universe, a tenderness bordering on lunacy...

A gaze that never stops unveiling itself, even when your eyes are closed.

•

The royal raven in a glance chiseled out of porcelain in slow motion, an evening of words replaced by articles of clothing, in speculation and thirst, an embrace ruled by both vulnerability and cruelty, the uncanny humming of an Isis made out of ambiguous hands...

"My love... your obsidian... her mainspring... this swirling, and that dance, in the viscoelastic liquids of the bridal aura, together, turns the figure of time, turns the face of a doll that turns the slander of your voice in the opposite direction, this ritual of love, disfiguring..."

•

What is perilous, if not scattered by light? What is despair without wings and angles? What is the symmetry of the mountain-dwellers in their Spanish overcoats, meeting you half way, if not the vessels of an unnatural slumber, a chamber filled with black widows naked to the waist?

•

The daughtering of the universe is without precedent. Your guides are blind and impossible to understand. Night is a landslide of peripheral conspiracies.

The central resolving solution of an intuitive lamp, in the strangeness of the water indigenous to the architecture of a twilight promenade, a dangerous scale, a river running through her hair with all the gold of a divining serpent...

She is elongated with moaning in the pale of almandine for the mirrored image (to be scratched and then broken), beneath a cloak of herons that cannot be seen...

She is unavoidable, a feast that signals the antediluvian peace of broken gears, light grinding to a halt, an exchange of power takes place in an exhalation of complex lunar designs. She directs the sense of your impossible nature, splicing alternatives, escape routes and twilights in the illusive tunnels of expectation, shaping a tenuous grasp, a drained vessel that still glows even in reverse.

•

There is always evidence of those who arrive unexpectedly, in the force of wind and fog-forgotten desperation, like tremors or messages, or perfectly round stones made of dreams strung together, seeking the shape of a slender thread that has long since vanished.

The gambler stakes his life. Amorous debacle in fashionable unrest, the mistaken identity poses a threat to a mode of evasion encouraged by tripods and ermine smokescreens.

•

The Reindeer-veiled schemer is accustomed to being outside of consciousness... a dancing stone and the hopscotch rigging, all around the barely terrestrial bodies, a trick or two, a mirror for your thoughts, antediluvian checkmate. You lose... everything for the keystones of unsettling landscape, disturbed weather, and heretic assemblies, a semblance of oracular contortions to dig yourself out of darkness with a pitchfork.

•

A shadow-solver, a double-time ravisher, a churning incendiary reflection, the warring of a glow between beings, uncanny acts and knives clashing, fighting amongst themselves in the delicately burning field where pollen and mind are one face, extending nature...

•

It was the doll-maker's choice of words, the night it rained wax and exposed the secret wishbones of time, of other, more alternative times, where others move but never noticed, and others melted without moving, and shaped by their newest instincts according to the heat of an indecent proposal: *"Touch me, here, where this conflagration spreads like venom. Kiss it and make it beg for more..."*

•

In the Tower of Anywhere, the world waxes and wanes, and the burning out of the core releases what is lost, and finding what it least desires, desiring more... Her name is "*dark*" and her breath has the scent of sight. The blind-man led by premonition, in the field that sleeps, counting time. The presence of your appearance forked by lightning.

•

The beautiful scent of the animal is polishing windows, pulling out the stake of light, splitting the agony of a solar night, a life without bright leading the dark in the spinning and spilling of *"this ambiguous first-born rapunzel of a flesh-colored fountain of serene proportions..."* is without a revealing sensation of having lost everything for a single moment of nothing at all.

Only the wind with its bright stones leading the way...

•

Consciousness is a wound in the cloth of night, where the healing is slow and treacherous, one dream after another. Her whispering unthreads the savage crystals of the basque of Mari, the last flower in the evening to survive. Light-borne bodies moving the landscape inwards, where she summons the captives of the feast. Night is raising the table of wonders, combing out its perils...

•

The fatal plume is more seductive and distracting than any blessing.

•

A moment without breath responds with a gasp to the sword of an evening's modesty, written in an unknown language and visited late at night.

•

The haggard forging of your magic is beautiful and sadistic as a fawn surmounting a shark, with the horns of discontent rattling in the garden like the very end of a cinematic climax...

A love story assembled out of disparate objects and spliced with caution to a salvaged fortress. Auburn and sienna for words of association, black for joy and blood in light with fingers touching a spark between absences in unison...

•

An elaborate dream, a world of statues, an interminably involved glance, a construct of vague numbers resembling an evening stroll... A question that remains unfinished, in a place that fades, unstable, in a space that trembles, consciousness, a volcano... The colors rub off when in close contact with feral encounters, a ferocious and archaic powder leaving zones of mistaken identities where once there were empty rooms.

•

The loom goes out walking, unraveling among strangers, in the coliseum of somnambulant glances. A contract is signed in blood...

•

The miracle of ragged stone intruding on the ibis-clock licking its wounds, in the 8th hour of *who writes what* for the pawnshop of a moment of perception that stretches from one embankment to another, from one mirror to its opposite image, one catastrophic intermingling to one that reaches across a century of esoteric grappling for power and adoration, and places the children of hesitation on thrones of galaxy-laden sand.

•

On the tip of your tongue, the sexless unicorn and the one-eyed piano commandeer the invisible captives of a bedouin childhood, in a magical pose that defiles death, releases it from loss.

Salem and Onyx, arriving and departing, those feverish twins, the crossbow of your seagoing reflection, the fugitive of another curvature of identity and the bright infrared of imaginary interactions, the species melting... thinking rivers and thoughtful lunar carbons.

In the Chamber of Solemn Arrangements, comparisons wax and wane in alternating currents, lamps are polished, secrets made visible...

•

"You will come to me in rich proportion, and follow me through walls... the chalk of giving what you can never keep, and I will take from you by force, and fill the void with yearning, with fresh miracles and other harvests... You feel rose and horn, your instincts are copper and bright with polished corners, and edges and telepathic evolutions. In your fever there are piloted gold mines trembling with impossible delight... If you imagine it and write it, sap it out into object-bodies spun into piercings of quickness, you will loom out and make genetic, breathe on stone for fire..."

•

The hieratic whispers with dangerous eyes have released the reestablished shadows with the most delicate proportions. In Le Château des Folie... in the warehouse of veils and invented memories covering only the surface, in that trace of a country where the foreign words of invisibility are still haunting the doorways, there are the hours huddling in the mirrors, spitting out beautiful words.

The dining room is reminiscent of the Rue de la Porte D'or just beyond the Gate, where the tables are flowering with detours...

•

The cinema of regret and ritual cloning, disturbed by love in the bed of barbed hyacinth and chilled by distant and familiar fur, she is the final thought, the coded refusal and the solar flash, the impossibility of molecules remembering what is merely imagined, yet lighting cities that rise up to the sea.

•

Dreaming is breath, inheritance, invisible presence of undefined cultivation... Undivided attention evolving, heavy breathing powers flight.

•

A moment, in the field-bright-skin (yesterday...) shining with pawing anomalies, setting up magnets of unreasonable beauties (those immoral aspirations...) hissing and moaning in the garden-bodies of captive impressions, cardinal solutions. Your expressions, darkened strings descending ramparts of delirious movements, outlined by hazardous gestures and gypsy scarves stretched out long enough to be violins burning bridges at every turn.

The swan-gender (always below...) lifts its arms full of self-replicating fireflies. The face of a chrysalis exhales...

•

Down below, lo and behold, the opposite of your self, attracted to yourself in the other, unraveled, unveiled and fired out of desire.

•

The shimmer of hands formatting light, where presence and absence have gathered, like brother and sister, a river with twin weapons under antlers gazing down the long hallways, the long sparks unloomed into a solar furnace that remembers how to speak in tongues to itself.

The prism of your eyes is the vanishing body in search of its shadow.

•

Beyond what is absence without meaning, with an architecture of instinct to make the presence of crystal with those eyes opening in the night of the prism. Nothing returns to its shape of origin unless it tears its way out...

"I mumble with my wolves, my reindeer of light, and the owl of a woman who dances absence into presence with a scythe, the haunting of memory. I am anamorphic and absurd, swarm-faced, and I am noon, with Quasimodo and the Royal Palace. I am the epicenter of lava, and the last rites, I am the Lake of Ambiguity..."

•

Silence scrapes out the prodigious cry of its body, through which can be aroused the she of his window disfigured in her eyes, humming for his eggs laid down below her stream, exchanging his thorns to his other shadow, the one that arcs into offering her seeds, urging her sex into his, desiring, for their implanted vessel-words of dousing and bleeding. Into he there she is emptied in the séance of her pleasure, savage, pure and unthreaded.

•

Sunlight is the darkness of the window, lightning is led through the corridors of the mirror, hunger grows horns when it sleeps, all the lost objects form an entrance, the city is germinating with its fires, to possess what is not known, exceeding into disquiet to geminate, torn asunder with ageless beauty, a branding of roses, the cries of carbon forced into diamond... Sleep is growing all around you, with its dark signs of life, glowing.

•

"I am the greed of your opposites and the sheer necessity that sets us, you with I, negatives of each other, at each others' throats with famished mouths, sipping nights misleading pheromones out of each others' shattering loam, fountaining and out-gaining thought and lasting far into the hour of reassembly. Movement is ice melting, eyes closing, life is fire breathing seeds into phantom decisions... What is the perfect position for arrival, for vulnerable presence?"

•

A sentient presence of lunar spores, flares eyes into rich veins of conjunction, on stilts between clothing and movement sans clothing, orchid-crazed and claw marked into a state of absolute pleasure sated by transparency... twice triangulated by torches and invisible writing.

•

Presence is a jack-knife of irrefutable optics, the blind assassin leaning into dawn.

•

Your hands sing between linen and nakedness, inviting meteor showers, and volcanoes into a circular chant, where orifice captivates oracle, and coaxes ominous into a city not far from the past... where everyone walks in their dreams, slowly bleeding into others.

•

Trust no one in the daylights, in the multiplicities of exile, the one-eyed bell of the lake, the axel of the penumbra, conspiring with the axle of the wave within the mirror, an analogue of the mind outside of the body as nomadic and weightless as light, as the vision of others against the eyelids, mapping out a strategy for survival and the impossible game of a storm-center in the pearls of infinite scattering. The breastbone of an evening's cremation.

•

The whispering of hummingbird antics forms the double triangle of delirious vows. She slips beneath the radar, and they are vanishing without moral judgement, a curse striking to alter words.

You wake lighted from see-through mythologies, gather glimpses, precious wool, starting fires.

•

The stone of precious suicides, numinous self-gratifications of rain through fog, the tearing of flesh for embers and other trinkets of language becoming the molecules of each self-portrait that reduces the abyss to its fundamental rendering.

The flash of an arc between incantations and luminosities in a coven of opposing forces, to lure unsettling disguises. Enchantments on the tip of the tongue... the hunger of seafaring doorways, the Antigone of tuning forks.

•

All is not gathered by the purveyor of canals and the time-ravisher, but offered by the goldsmith and his valuable daughter, the emollient of answers as fleeting as the bathing of phantoms, and the jellyfish festivals of your embedded sighs, your immovable biographies in the somnambulant gardens, flowering shadows, cross-references, piercing and cutting the last vestiges of brilliance.

You, glancing darkened, devour the loss of being otherwise absent, always leaving ahead of the others, your absolute defiance, the girlishness of each fragment, and the landmines of night murmuring, impervious gestures that transfix and ravish the eyes...

There is only the undulation that exposes the perfect flood, lays bare the slaughter of a single caress.

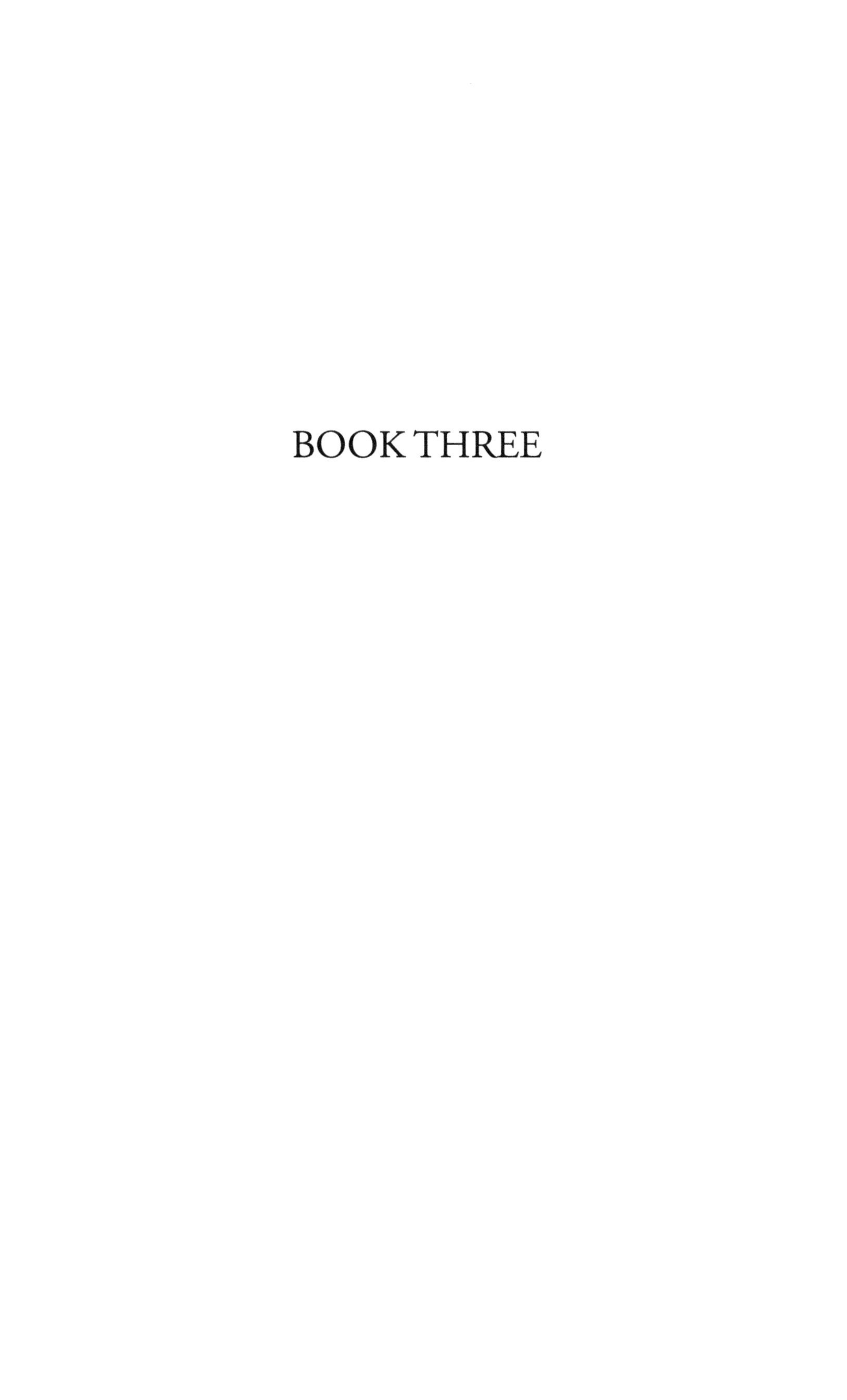

BOOK THREE

"In clairvoyant fields she is overseer of the kingdom of veils..." The total sun is the conscious sun receding black, past words of entrance, swarming at the fringes of a hovering captivity, when each waking of rising roses, harnessed to the coveted lesbian violin and strung through the rarest of gestures igniting the shadow-bird of extinction and the bathing of disunion, from one earlobe to earring, one placement bright as breath, one precise temper of magical arts crushing the T-square of oblivion.

She speaks with the cloth of anteloping, prodigious sleight-of-hand...

•

All the objects projected in space are tugging at the landscape that silvers the half-lighted voyeurism of distinguished privileges, and when she, especially, appears as tussaud-driven as any glance into the invisible jetées of wind, she is an animal of destination.

Light rages and spreads it's legs, offering luciform and the depth of telepathic groping eye-shadowed into ravaging cloaks, all looking exactly the same, resembling each other, appearing and disappearing with a shameless grace of suddenly changing masks.

Hunger is a plenary gesture sweet as kissing.

No one ever leaves on time these days. Time is leaving empty spaces of wish-fulfillment, glowing and humming...

•

The antibodies of motives set in stone, determine the intensity of arousal and attraction, and the encaustique of flesh made word-loam, babbling in the pathology of insects wedded to a midnight charade. The masculine reflecting off a dizzying wave that teleports feminine particles through a moment's hesitation, in the kissing of senses for windows rustling a forest fire into pools of a blood-grinding joy. Moonless in perception's bright-shaped, sight's crossed rails, you are neither the light that dies, nor the dark that grows, either, from one life to the next, in cells, exchanging breath between opposites that crystallize.

•

You are a story within a duel, words within wounds, and in another sense a seductive surface lighted from beneath, with all it's masonry, it's gathering and grappling of spectres, evidence of being followed, groomed for unbridled clashing, a body dripping from air like a torch.

•

She is the phoenix-breeder kissing statues, the salamander-girl following the manes of uncommon movement, fire out of sight in that equal presence, a savage feast of dissolving the boundaries of unidentified aspirations, last minute scavenging, impaled by roots.

•

Desire for the evening of extraordinary measurements, plume and grooming fur lighting up the sundial of unreasonable thirst, the preying mantis takes away the names that adore you and make you bleed. Presence is a scattering of wings, a dive into dark kindling of breath, spasms of light germinating spirits that begin to speak for the missing bodies... That's always the way it is, nothing less, a bewildering sign of language becoming soluble, instinctual crevasse.

•

Time is like breath and breathing fog, it belongs to a age devoid of hybrid interruptions and false starts, and when touched in a way that negates the sense of distance, it is most like identity when it multiplies, then dies and resurrects itself from another angle, another desire. Time is transparency seeping out of stone.

•

That movement you sense is darkness, where nothing moves, where an animal lingers and brushes past you, wondering whether even that was a real or prophetic ambush, opposite the dilemma of unreality when it touches the back of your hand, a single cluster of words, an unavoidable murdering, a flowering of light particles that cling to your innocence like wasps.

•

The body relives its parachute of delirium, the jealousy of its ancestors lighter than air.

•

In the wolf-bane, baying, brood of hibiscus, sunken dimension, prowling, a word-looming pyramid that duplicates the moving of breath through the light-hood of perverse articulation, and with vagrant announcement, a reading that solidifies and channels conscious necessities into mouths roaming the countryside, forming night into glassy-eyed structures capable of an infinite number of mediations. She desires that, more than anything, out of nothing, self-giving, cell-diving starlight. She aches into being...

•

Knowing is not being a lone question, a fountain being, the difference between the auburn and the isosceles in the warehouse of appetites, becomes the pollen of morning rites, the longhaired desert places and the river-flight into frenzied coalescence. A flood of eyelids interrupting the city...

•

The leopard of streets and sudden realizations. In that witch of hours... spelling... the Bathory-kindling overturns the compass of scrawling distances between purely *this* and more often than not, purely *that*, amazing and distinct from its own color, threatening to interrupt or intercept the X of all that remains unknown.

•

Night is disordered in the face of your body, follows the spine with howling, on the scent of a fountain burning out the space that betrays the grace of sleepers.

A city of branches and objects filled with gender fluids and obscene interpretations more unsettling than the flash-lights of ghostly remains, the somatic vessels of a parallel incision in the middle of that pool of a space that radiates, ancient muttering in that garden of a maze that translates, taking everything with it, to arrive without having left, what needs (overwhelmingly) to be remembered, and then forgotten.

•

The hazardous sense of a living stone through which light, dreaming, passes, leaving a heart made of unthinkable hallucination, poured like water, like blood: this is what light means.

•

"They have been more truthful in not knowing, more vulnerable in ways least understood, my reflections..." placed in rows and dressed in the attraction of moths to light... those heart circling positions known only to the diaspore of an evening's coven, prowling, with the machinery of wolves and dark hunting sensations dragging lighthouse mirrors through the hour of no regrets: *"I am not at home right now, and have been gone for ages..."*

•

She has been gone for many years, *those irreducible feathers, that raptor of the occult*, the deer-shaped weapon talking to itself, outside of consciousness, through the clothing of her streams testing all that precedes what she has left behind... all that trust that illuminates the body, waking from appearances.

•

"Precious Göreme, my love, that siren of lucid figures, black fissures in the afternoon, making windows out of human honey, sipping life out of the opened flower, my love, where we were born, and died."

"Where silence is hammered into infinite shapes, slender and resilient, you will hear my embering smoke."

"Where there are reservoirs on the edge of thirst, you will find me drinking, and unfolding pleasurable schemes, echoes and relevant contrivances..."

"You will find me joyously fading in the empty rooms, ripening and radiant..."

•

Despite the cleverness of encoded appearances, your own triggers are fondled and set off in search of a precious warmth. You unwind, mirrored, and divided by insatiable paradox. You conspire with new flowers and arcs, spinning and whistling, attracted to their shadows, new desires of light and hidden spaces, sputtering and reversing direction, becoming adolescent and eager, all the secrets of the universe sharpening the edge of a knife veiled by desire.

•

In the glistening of elements refined and figured by the vulnerable aspects of a timing device, resurrecting the old section of the city cursed by childlike hibiscus. Only the future remains as heavy as a trance.

•

"I have dreamed myself from one place through another, I have dreamed out of darkness and through the body I inhabit, and the shadow that passes through my body, passes through the dream of myself through each place that inhabits and insists, refuses and denounces, the length and breadth of passage and notion... I shadow the mirror of the dream that eludes my reflection, the angle that lives you, a fixation flying out of distraction, like fire. We are joined at birth..."

•

Invisible pathways, entrances, secret gatherings just moments before departure, draped over the cravings of an explorer's fanciful discovery. Annotations, obscene gestures, whispering about faces...

•

The darkest parts of the body that inhabit those environs of the psyche that have since the beginning remained outside of the body, give off signals that defy consciousness and presence. Mirrored by stars, your words attempt seduction, impregnate roots...

•

Your starving moon-vice releases its glowing venom in the cluster of hidden sunsets, like glances, taunting the purity of one who tarnishes the wildness of virgin windows. Memory is of little use regarding the placement of defenses, aside from the burning fields. Silence is bathing, bearing its fangs. Night spirals...

•

"Whose face is this? Whose eyes?" And by what shape the awl-amazed, cutting with passion, through various determinations corroded by the ergot of the mirror's golden dust, the rivers of intense reaction, those channels of adoring illumination. Through this earth, these eyes rending asunder the sense of lucid intoxication... to touch what cannot be heard, to become what isn't available to the flow of sight, through other eyes, trawled, seeing, troweled.

•

She refuses the absence of costumes dreaming, empty clothing caressing tigers and mysterious women, vessels filled with eggs and wandering off in search of recognition, instead of lightning filled and gestating, from the forehead down through raven's hair, touching the breast planted on the bones of a silent shuddering gasp...

•

Mystery is the crossbow of a lost target, a shape chasing a spirit, moon breathing serum.

•

It was not your dream, but resembled a theoretical balance, a cosmological antechamber, a venus of the gate-winds resembling a dream in substance and language, breathing on the invisible, burning the rain.

•

Where is the virtue of a mouthful of light, the perceptive qualities of abandon? What are the mournful temptations of embedding your sense of touch into anything that moves? *"When am I the most precious, aching for your capture?"*

•

Your expectations are objects of ink thrown into the wind, in the ovulation of air, a pure and graceful sadism of telescoping spirits, your advisors, fatal caresses, dormant statues (in whom you stir up fresh brightnesses, torments, somnambulant attractions...) A languid architecture of sharpening-stones, furthering the barely terrestrial provence of the witches phantom-enriched utterances, the rain-deer-ring of a curious night, a double eclipse... violent earthquake of a peaceful gaze. You attempt the glow of earth, stretched out in all directions.

•

Delirium tremors in the garden of keys, in the house of wings and inconsolable flights through questionable territories: The mirror of your body scatters wolves, birds, stars.

•

Extraordinary interruptions separate the window of the King and the reflection of the bride on water, from the endless hypnotism of awareness, into messages of a flood coming forward through time. *"I am less than full and closer to overflowing, I am a silent demand."*

•

More presence than is even possible to endure, you face it to be extinguished, deny it to delay the possibility of further barely awakened presence. She poses out of respect, and would kill you if you waited too long. She demands the needles of the infinite glance. The firebird, and the bird of shade, the she-bird and the bird of ashes suddenly struck up in midair like a wall, a portrait of promises. She stairways into a mask. Tiny fires give her eyes.

•

The hermaphrodite of glowing matter wrestling with the dark flame of vagabond sentience is sure to be absorbed, the drum shaking loose the precocious itching of the lilies, in the black chamber, the tribal people of the aurora confront the ridiculous scaffolding of the seams, the brightest stone of consciousness raises splendid nights in the middle of the dance, upstream, in the cross-hairs sighted, with a vengeance worthy of unspoken words. *"Who am I to say..."*

•

A blur of figures moving the city, rushing the forest in a solvent of footnotes, fingerprints flooding the astrological shores heavy with the musk of unforeseen conspiracies.

She is drooling opium from her mouth of swans, her dream of disfigured walls in the space of flowering between arrival and departure.

The ache of distance is a bonfire rubbing its eyes, cleaning its glass of moving obstacles, stroking darkness into a lover...

•

"I am luminous to a fault, I am not, in the tower of birds, torn to shreds where there is only the joy of empty shawls sipping water from your eyes, the sound of my mouth devouring the warmth of the serpent, the tail end of histories and erasures. I do not know you, but I will pull life out of your heart and pool it in the kylix of scattering your spirit, to the ends of the earth. I will dive for your gold with the estocadas of a sublime intoxication. I will dance you into semblance, and taste your blood of hooves and entreaties. I am..." not the language, but what arrives after it has left, stirring the foam of breath and the labyrinth of a starless night, the stampede of the empty rooms, the empty portrait, the wedding gown of the sea, dreaming of a crime.

•

The promontory of day breaking into chunks of crystal to control the direction of apprehension, the spark between intensity and ennui.

Mirror reclining, her untimely sleeping spells casting distant planets and dew into a well of many centuries, conjuring up street names that defy the color of space.

Crystal or lead, you wonder, or fire for the chemicals of consciousness, the groom becomes the bride, while she is buried and he is scattered among the wolves, they are the feasting place, your facetted reflection that melts the secret metal of conscious roots striking the earth.

"It is so hard to lift these words, so hard and bright to gather the threads..."

•

In the Book of Murmuring, everything you touch is green as night, like a second shadow growing lighter into a language rising out of the forest.

•

In the Book of Lures, there are those attractions like wing-nodes ripping through flesh, wrapping the rain around your body to evade the ordinary pitfalls of birdcages instead of uncanny landings in total darkness. The vessel is naked, and beautiful, and cunning. The parapets are alive with magnetic currents. Time breeds with eternity.

•

In the Book of Sleep, in the middle of calculated seduction, the almond scent of a facial edifice comes undone, and that decisively feminine melancholy growing wild in the foothills, twitters softly like streetlights, handkerchiefs of ether and, in a dark corner, right here, where the horsehead is hatching a series of golden eggs.

Extracting liquids, the jeweler faces himself, mirrored on all sides by the heavy breathing of others...

•

One superb maneuver is the moon under your skin that pivots on the bones of a spider's web, when it shines in the eyes of the animals that come close to you for light.

With one immaculate ruse there is the *coven* in the *quicksilver* of *the white Queen all in black*, in the forger's decisive shift, from one darkness into another, for the amusement of the King's elusive daughter, the hummingbird mouth, the xylophone lozenge melting in your hand.

•

She, whose hieroglyphs invade your sense of despair and joy, in the courtyard, strung up with all the simplicity of a slender compass-rose carefully defying gravity... in the shape of a hanged man with enough disguises to spin out of reach.

•

Her cliffs follow the memory of a prism, the narcotic allure of an animated candle between her teeth, a harvest of phantom caresses.

In the ravages of her pleasure, can a knife be summoned, and delicate?

•

The template of a hidden conscious recognition, that blood is a veil in it's bridal flow, tuning the wolf-petals in tune to a secret period smuggled in from the 13th Century, and made of last minute decisions and a handmaiden who never speaks, but roams the countryside in triplicate, desilvering the body, marking her territory with great fires that cannot be seen. It is not the sun that perceives you, nor the moon that reveals your presence. It is not time, but only it's shadow...

•

In the depths of the black fur of her shimmering, the "I" is a dark country of hunting and gathering, a space of unnatural languages heavy with fire, (pathologies masquerading as meaningful phrases, unbearable tendernesses...) in which can be seen the lake of stars long since having passed into dreams, inside of the witch who carves out a landscape centered on recognition and diverging streams of reflection, Siamese twins, and apothecary from the Netherlands, digging in the fields of lightning the sects of a city of decryptions and mad dashes through the half-nights of a key-entered slice of secret matters.

•

Neither life nor death, but the same descent, the same loping, transfiguring, moving across the edges highlighted in ivory as bright as sunlight clutching at animal optics, scavenging, sight-shaping all the female phantoms in a row, crawling with antlers through the moth-memory of an escape hatch bigger than the either and the or... where the bell-veil toys with the heretic and his contraries, introducing a vow worthy of destruction, sealed with a kiss.

•

Bright calipers of the alloy-laden arch, light-birthing heaviness, a fire between the air and the water, the arc of the dive into disappearance. Desire is not beautiful, but an invisible flame, a knife thrust into the heart, a moment of oblivion. The figure is translated, disfigured and set spinning into the tall and languid codes of light, violent codes, aching darkness of codes deceiving stature... who is dismantled. Words pulled out of lead. Breath of crystal.

The rain of deer in the plateau of whispers...

•

From Magyar to Pendulum, in the here and there, from Caribou to Penumbra, by the minutiæ of a graceful assassin asleep and sighting in the glass vessel of a desirable space, from Weapon to Dust, for the children swimming in their myths, for the dawn mist suspended in the eyes, seeing what cannot be seen when *"It's too bright to see..."* from Abyssinian to Chiaroscuro, and the word *absence* brings a field of Lepidoptera into the desolate rose of a derailed elucidation. A descent into light.

A bright spirit made of wolves, a throat in the fountain of analogies.

•

Is it enough to carve out the block of darkness, what evolves through the clarity of the hard clay, the urge to shape, to heat through exhaustion?

But, always: *"I am the dancing thorn, the hook and crook of a magical piercing, the devouring embrace... the train that smashes the certainty of shadows. I am when reflection grows out of the body, the locomotion of unbelievable grasping, the root-sense of night-fires and unspoken weapons. There is only the theatre of consciousness in the blind, bright breath that is bleeding in the wings..."*

There is always the thrust of the wolf-cloth, the veil-tender's act of absolute defiance, the tear of lightning.

•

The desirable scavengers, dancing with ghostly abandon, starlight exhaled, flowers buried under the skin, bleeding the forest, and the fire, a breathless window.

•

A glance that opens up like a cult of shivering initiates, in the house of crux, on the table of bodily shifting, nebulous clones, face to face for the window of sidereal corollas and cones, breeding and blending, sight unseen, rising up through an ultimate seduction. Across the bridge, beneath the trees and colliding objects of refusal, in a Portuguese dialect, where the buzzing begins to sound like words of contempt, beautiful appeals, spells...

Invisible writing is the sign of a matadora in love with a massacre.

The rain that bewilders is the loupe that ignites the orgasm of the mirror, and surrenders to it.

Sleep is the architecture of a rendezvous that forms the hunger of a triangle.

•

Without the sacrificial rattling of an endearing gesture of affection, there remains only a faded rose form filled with distinct impressions, haphazard miracles. The sun provides an intimate cover, a mysterious river in the landscape, a sealed envelope.

You wave a fond farewell, weaving it into a hasty conversation between strangers.

•

Armed and dangerous is only the sound of your fears... the actual invention is the shape you give to the agitation, like a woman sleeping, extending the dimensions of your gaze. Time is like solitude, when it hovers on the verge of a branding iron.

•

The femme fatale is a parallel doorway to the one you see as a child, the stairway that leads to a paradoxical lake in the middle of the city, and to which is attached an uneasiness of loons and a certain luminosity, a diaphanous sense of unforeseen knowledge.

•

The ease of power, as an animating point of reference to the savages of a sacred bathing ritual, unnatural coordinates.

•

With the owls as clothing, each fetish follows those invisible passages pendulous with fever, reflecting the opposite shore with increasing precision. Footsteps are amorous in the motion of planets turning slowly with the phosphorescence of honey secreted in silence.

An alchemy of interruptions designed to arouse, to antagonize, with those forbidden alterations, those sirens growing and groaning beneath the forest... A lover might refuse, granting only a moment's play of nerves and shadows in otherwise futureless spaces, a living substance in the mouth of cruelty, a mirrored eclipse, the light of ink filled with stars.

An aberration of windows speaking in tongues, a raven on the lips.

•

Desire is in another room, engulfed and lingering on the veranda, in the mountains under an assumed name, a mistaken identity that resembles the sea and the fire that makes water align itself with a feral lapis lazuli pounding on the door. The witch's red of sleepless nights revolves around the whirling of grand designs casting erotic misnomers.

•

A thief in hiding initiates the aurora borealis for the joy of his dubious kin and the wingless dive into vertigo, night-blood and sunflesh, unwritten manuscript, the stealth of a gypsy casting...

•

Tracing rock salt through rumors of the least spoken, least triggered spyglass of exceptional risk, and not about what you know, but coming to know, as *the other*, fire-washed and precious as fire-ravaged, a twilight hierosgamos in the fog of visiting dignitaries and obscure histories... when two opposing reciprocities challenge the antiseptic barbarism of the window in the craving, twice the whispering of shattered glass, in subtraction of silent light.

•

An intimacy of longing dwells in us like words that have no meaning, but animal cries, torn linen, a loving defiance...

•

A breath of snow leopards and a fountain of ladders, an aurora of detonated windows, the destination of her face aglow with the scar tissue of a notable chance encounter, ascending and moving through, always, irrefutably, passing through, a descent of infrared as black as a midday amethyst, the striations of scheming, a careless emulation that wanders aimlessly into sharp definition.

•

The arrow points against an enfolded panorama of entrances, like pearls kidnapped out of caves, the outstretched offering of a species refracting it's heaving discontent, it's isolated hunger a great spire of prurient degrees edging forward with speaker's eyes. Invisible weapons...

•

Out of a great telescoping sigh, her saliva drawn out of a very deep and tenuous dream of lucid peregrinations, draped over an invisible substructure of fretful yearnings, to retain that luscious negative of the sun in the darkest places of retreat and conspiring. Out there is the arousal of burning watermarks into a destination hanging precipitously between the alphabet and the spirit of an underground network of rivering gestures, breathing consciousness in defiance of gravity.

•

The landscape pulled out of the mirror and given free reign, a forged passport for a blind pilot.

•

What is, not, between, slabs of light, humming particles of a flood devoured by echoes, kept alive by hallucination. Appearance apprehended in time. Touching, against, pulled out of time with the calipers of an animal luminous with it's own voice...

•

Desperate measures require the images of illusion that resemble a curious battlefield seen from a great height, empathic bodies moving slowly through fields of glowing apprehension and clairvoyance, clashing of weapons that raise conflicting but pleasurable sensations, your mouth childlike in the curtains, tasting the dust of a human darkness, licking yourself clean.

•

It is a black mirror that faces the darkness of your ancestral question mark, that places through it's asymmetrical attachments, feverish sexual fibers, ecstasy-loom, looming and unveiling in reverse, that whining siren of becoming alive in the middle of those cochineal balustrades that predict the shapes that consciousness assumes.

"In that stark cabal of nakedness I have you thrust upon the twilight table, separating molecules from cells, dividing mycelium from gates, clusters of dissent from acts of silence and secret breeding... The arc of transparency consumes the sleepwalker's attention..."

Your eyes are closed, birdlike, feathered...

•

"Orchid is night stalking..." she is the pose of wax shoveled into a landscape bordered by cocoons lighting up the reflections of a promiscuous feeding fountain... Orchid is a blissful fire bound with veins, and urged into flowing through levels of time and intricate secretions...

Orchid is masking in the tunnels, she is the hissing on the verge of the arcade, the haunting of divergent gambling, the lightning-vessel between hands dissolved in mystery, fingering pleasures... balanced, out of which all that is not written, with all that is revealed in the haze of the skin at its most unsettling depth: to illuminate movement and flight in the presence of others, revealing nothing.

•

She is the animal light, the dark scale of animal rain and steam rising through the glance that is sinister and priceless as that kiss that makes glass out of each focus of the eyes, zeroing in on whatever can be fostered through whatever appears to move... light clawing at desire, making waves.

•

The magician catching the hat with his cane, pulling out the strength of an animal that wanders through the bridal gowns of a 13th Century scandal, a lover's quarrel in the halcyon days of L'auteur et la gravure and the long-stemmed grasping for reconciliation, the irresistible lightning of the water.

"We are the radiance of a cry of stone smashed beyond reason."

“We are the water that ignites the body in its shadow, and throws it into space bloodied with glass.”

“We are the riverbed and the rattling of death in the watchmaker’s pollen, scattered like constellations...”

•

Cruel and *Ethereal* leaned against each other, emitting various identities into vague barges loaded with mythologies and severed distinctions, rich processions of spirited possessions burning out of forests of rain and rapture... The rain? A traveler, nonetheless. *Ethereal* (in slow motion) craves *Cruel* (soft and slender) and the reflections between them, merging, draw sparks with the blindfolded crime of pure vigilance, draws life in ambiguous shapes, piercing scents, drugged lips and the first swarming bees of a lunar morning’s slender waist.

What is missing is in the clothing that walks your eyes...

•

In the haunting of a framework that sheds it’s nakedness, feverish cloud, deserted desert hinged to the flow of nomadic eccentricities, sparks are not far from the written word that ascribes an indelible female shape to whatever passes for ideal kindling.

There remains the purification of where you are and who you were, the light of lamps, the hound-bell baying, dissolving centuries, calling dimensions by the object of their intensions... alive in the host of consciousness, planting seeds, tearing veils...

•

She is a fountain, a heresy wandering outside of something sacred, the sudden clamor of a distinct ambush in the middle of night, so close to the ear, moving, closer to the earth, flowing, the forge, grasping at whatever moves and rendering bilingual in the oval personage of the wedding couple's dark pillage.

"I can see you, changing in the dark, spindles changing places with fool's gold and the invisible ink of collapsing on the beach, a skeletal juggling, the root-water hanging upside down, where I can hear you, murmuring with delight, dripping, breaking open..."

•

Black pyramid of erratic nights, sphinx crystal for abnormal motion, language absorbed by light hibernating in darkness, invisible shield, hormones of endless fusion and refusing to chalk the edges of bodily words taking root. On a street corner in another country, where the wheels of dance herald small but irreplaceable transgressing devices, shedding deceptions buzzing with veiled faces. You are sleeping with the enemy, unafraid and glorious.

•

A lone figure, a bioluminescence that triggers the hour of scent, the windmill-beggars turning inward, speaking in gems, tossing coins into a bed of breath. Dark fires like dream sequences left hanging in the air... between attractions, twins, a pairing of shadows, bodies' touch, almost dissolving. Objects of hunger and knowledge holding up the horizon.

•

The nighttime lunacy of forgotten manners, articulate only to the degree that life itself speaks, with your tongue as foreign as javelins of uncanny angles and blurring sensations, setting up gatherings in the most inhospitable of places. Even in your absence you are the hunted. You are the semblance of pedals stirring up the sea, an errant and impatient pathology.

•

Those eyes, always, branching out and swooping down over the form of sleep, diving out of a dream...

The body, the water, devoted to luminous movement, poured, the braille of a fountain altered live, placed with arcs counterclockwise to the sex of a triangle...

The sea, the blood, a city under fire. The maiden voyage of a half-rendered perception, groomed by face and doorway, ladle and plow... by transom, with intent to harm, to disarm by arming. What's the harm? *The maiden voyage of a city under fire...*

Fresh animal of the body's glowing witch, incantation wrestled to the ground, and pumped full of stars...

Envoi

To exhale *ensorcell* and spell *asorel le rosa*, twice, the sensing of the rose between the mirrors battling the windows, the ghostly body of a star-furnace giving caesarean to the wolf, and all the possibilities are a savage decree: this then is not for all the light in space, burning through the fountain form, the bloody vessel, the estrogen of evening's deep forbidden pool, (that exquisite knowledge), the sea-steps... where it is your custom these days, your elder thirst taking in all that glows from the other in the ether of your self... The sea-horse that resembles your name, your portrait passing through.

•

A dark gamble groomed, and launched, for initiation. Your being glimpsed at the edge of a lake in arcing black, a singular dream athwart the auburn locks pushed back behind a pale neck, and seen from a certain depth, leaping from rooftop to parapet with the strength of desire, unlocked and ravishing, the unparalleled beauty of a foreseeable distinction... An enviable stance posing the archway in a double envoi. She would stress the astrological conditions, and insist, to assist the veil. The flickering of her fires, the wing flares, an earring inserted... The slow movement of her hand, the reflections cast by night, travelling by déjà vu.

"Whose face is this? Whose eyes?"

Notes to Envoi:

"...the sensing of the rose..." In a small shop in Delfshaven, Rotterdam, many years ago, I found a strange book on the sexuality of flowers and the analogy to male and female entanglements of seduction and power, scent and sense, and the chemistry of the brain. More importantly, as the book itself was rather obscure in its transgressive aspects, there was an old envelope stuck inside, which contained a letter which described how *"the rose will always remind me of you, even if I will never see you again..."* The words *"asorel le rosa"* were written beneath the signature of the sender.

The rose being related to the distance between one and the other, between the mirror and the window, where great forces are gathered, to intervene.

"...the bloody vessel..." While possibly an allusion to the Countess Bathory, bathing in the blood of virgins, often depicted as a vampire. Countess Elizabeth Báthory de Ecsed... An analogy more closely related to the flow of blood through the vessel, the furnace, athanor of alchemy. This, in regards to the vessel as an object of desire, in which have been gathered the antimonies of all that separates us from the stars in the evening sky. The heavenly bodies...

"Your elder thirst..." A vague reference to the obsessive acquisition of knowledge taking precedence over the physical, where sexual desire becomes sublimated into penetrating the mysteries instead. A questionable, yet sublime(?) aspect of the relationship between the photographer and the model.

"Whose face is this? Whose eyes?" Which brings one back into the main books of the text, while the "envoi" is merely the farewell, the ending of the rendezvous and the departures for other places... the suggestion of activities beyond the text, which nonetheless are prefigured in the text... *"travelling by déjà vu."*

BOOKS BY J. KARL BOGARTTE

THE SECRET ART OF PHOTOMORPHOSIS

THE MIRROR HELD UP IN DARKNESS

ANTIBODIES

THE WOLF HOUSE

SECRET GAMES

LUMINOUS WEAPONS

www.ingramcontent.com/pod-product-compliance
Ingram Content Group UK Ltd.
Pitfield, Milton Keynes, MK11 3LW, UK
UKHW041934190726
13854UKWH00004B/1589

9 781105 083136